INTRODUCING THE STAR OF THIS BOOK

★ STEGOSAURUS ★

(ST...-russ)

DID YOU KNOW...

that *Stegosaurus* is described as having a body almost the size of a bus, a head the size of a horse and a brain the size of a walnut! Sounds rather bizarre, but read on to find out how this rather odd combination worked...

Stegosaurus means 'roof lizard'

SETTING THE SCENE

It all started around 231 million years ago (mya), when the first dinosaurs appeared, part-way through the Triassic Period.

The Age of the Dinosaurs had begun, a time when dinosaurs would rule the world!

Scientists call this time the

MESOZOIC ERA
(mez-oh-zoh-ic)

and this era was so long that they divided it into three periods.

TRIASSIC
←········ lasted 51 million years ········→

JURASSIC
←········ lasted 56 million years ········

252 million years ago

201 million years ago

Stegosaurus lived during the Jurassic Period from 154 – 148 million years ago.

CRETACEOUS

lasted 79 million years

145 million years ago

66 million years ago

WEATHER REPORT

The world didn't always look like it does today. Before the dinosaurs and during the early part of the Mesozoic Era the land was all stuck together in one supercontinent called Pangaea. Over time, things changed and by the end of the Jurassic Period the land looked like this.

JURASSIC 150 mya

Named after the Jura Mountains in the European Alps

TRIASSIC

Very hot, dry and dusty

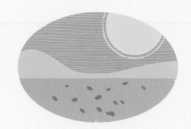

JURASSIC

Hot, humid and tropical

CRETACEOUS

Warm, wet and seasonal

As the land split apart more coastlines appeared. The weather changed from dry to humid and many of the deserts changed into lush rain forests

HOMETOWN

Here's what's been discovered so far and where...

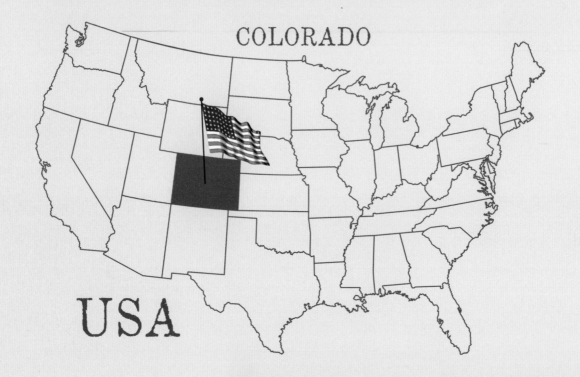

COLORADO

USA

PALAEONTOLOGIST
OTHNIEL CHARLES MARSH
NAMED STEGOSAURUS
IN 1877

Several partial skeletons, with spikes and plates. A skeleton nicknamed 'Sophie', is a young adult which is around 85% complete and is on permanent display at the Natural History Museum, London.

One of the most popular and iconic dinosaurs. The bones of *Stegosaurus* have mostly been found in Colorado, Wyoming, and Utah, USA, but one specimen was discovered near Batalha in Portugal.

Palaeontologists have identified four or five different species of *Stegosaurus*, so far.

VITAL STATISTICS

During the Jurassic Period the plant life became more varied and so there was plenty for the herbivores, the plant-eating dinosaurs, to eat. As a result they got bigger and bigger!

Stegosaurus
3.5m tall from its toes to the top of its plates

Let's look at *Stegosaurus* and see what's special, quirky and downright amazing about this dinosaur!

Having plates
on its back made
Stegosaurus look
taller and perhaps
more intimidating!

More about these
special plates later...

Door
2m high

STEGOSAURUS

Length: up to 9 m

Height: 3.5 m to the top of the spikes

Weight: 3.5 – 4 tonnes

BUS Traditional double deck

4.5 m high 11 m long 8 tonnes (empty) 2.5 m wide

11

ELEPHANT Average African elephant
3.5 m high 6 m long 5 tonnes

MOUSE

SCARY
SCALE

How does *Stegosaurus* rate?

NOT SCARY

| 1 | 2 | 3 | 4 | 5 |

When
wandering
around and
eating

If attacked,
Stegosaurus
would have
probably
swung its
immense tail
wildly!

| 6 | 7 | 8 | 9 | 10 |

S C A R Y

BRAININESS

When dinosaurs were first discovered
they were thought to be quite stupid!

Then a few scientists thought that some dinosaurs had
a second brain close to their butt! That's now just a myth.

Today scientists know that dinosaurs had one brain and were
intelligent for reptiles. Some were among the most intelligent
creatures alive during the Mesozoic Era, although
still not as smart as most modern mammals.

By looking at the:

Body size

Size
of the
brain

Sense
of
smell

Eyesight

Scientists can tell how they rated against each other...

WHERE DOES STEGOSAURUS, A PLANT-EATING DINOSAUR, STAND ON THE 'BRAINY SCALE'?

TROODON
(TRU-oh-don)

$^{10}/_{10}$
CARNIVORE

ALLOSAURUS
(AL-oh-SAW-russ)

$^{8}/_{10}$
CARNIVORE

IGUANODON
(ig-WAHN-oh-DON)

$^{6}/_{10}$
HERBIVORE

STEGOSAURUS
(STEG-oh-SAW-russ)

$^{4}/_{10}$
HERBIVORE

ANKYLOSAURUS
(an-KIE-loh-SAW-russ)

$^{3}/_{10}$
HERBIVORE

DIPLODOCUS
(DIP-lod-oh-CUSS)

$^{2}/_{10}$
HERBIVORE

These dinosaurs are drawn to
scale in relation to each other!

SPEED-O-METER

With long, pillar-like hind limbs and short
forelimbs, *Stegosaurus* wasn't built to run!
It has been estimated that *Stegosaurus*
probably achieved a top speed of around
a whopping 4 mph – yes, very slow!

SLOW

1   2   3   4   5

FAST

WEAPONS 8/10

As the herbivores grew, so did the predators that preyed on them. Being slow and heavy meant that *Stegosaurus* needed all the help it could get to survive an attack!

Instead of running away from trouble, *Stegosaurus* would have probably stood its ground and defended itself with its powerful tail, swinging it wildly, hoping to fend off an attack. It had four large, solid spikes at the end, called the thagomizer.

TAIL SPIKES

ARMOUR PLATES

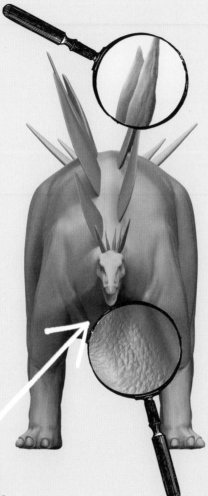

THROAT ARMOUR

has been found on some specimens. It may have been restricted to males or females, or perhaps it was something that developed with age.

Stegosaurus means 'roof lizard' and it was given this name by Othniel Charles Marsh as he thought that the plates lay flat on its back. Scientists now know that they stood upright in two rows.

Despite being their most striking feature, there is still a lot of discussion about what the plates were used for!

They could have been for:

- protection to stop other dinosaurs jumping on its back and intimidation to make it look bigger

- controlling body temperature, by turning towards and away from the sun

- attracting a mate!

TEETH

Stegosaurus had a toothless horny beak and very small, leaf-shaped 'cheek' teeth which it used to grind up food.

It seems likely that *Stegosaurus* had the ability to move its jaw up and down for basic chewing; scientists are still studying this.

Stegosaurus may have had cheeks, giving it space in its mouth to chew and fit in more food before swallowing. With a very small head and mouth, cheeks were very useful as it needed to eat a lot to survive.

 Tooth to scale

1 cm

Over-sized version of the tooth so you can see the detail

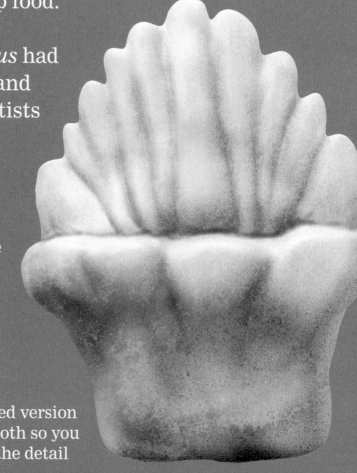

DIET

Stegosaurus could only raise its head one metre off the ground, so it would have fed on low-lying plants such as ferns, cycads and horsetails.

The bite force of *Stegosaurus* was less than that of a Labrador dog! Although it didn't have a particularly strong bite, it could strip plants with its horny beak.

Who lived in the same
NEIGHBOURHOOD?

CERATOSAURUS
(SER-at-oh-SAW-russ)

There were lots of predators living in the same neighbourhood as *Stegosaurus*, like *Ceratosaurus*.

This 6 m long predator had a big head with a horn on the nose and large, bladed teeth which suggest it hunted large prey. The horn was probably used for display.

ALLOSAURUS

(AL-oh-SAW-russ)

One of the largest meat-eating dinosaurs of its time, *Allosaurus* was the most common carnivore found in the same place as *Stegosaurus*.

It has been suggested that *Allosaurus* may have hunted in groups, a serious attack for any *Stegosaurus* to fend off!

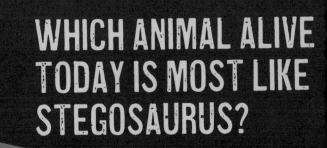

WHICH ANIMAL ALIVE TODAY IS MOST LIKE STEGOSAURUS?

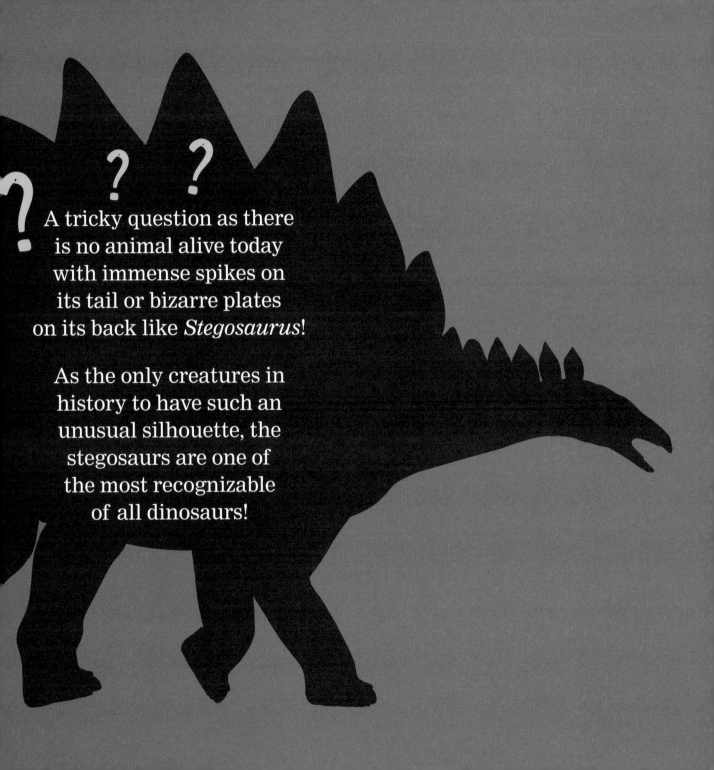

A tricky question as there
is no animal alive today
with immense spikes on
its tail or bizarre plates
on its back like *Stegosaurus*!

As the only creatures in
history to have such an
unusual silhouette, the
stegosaurs are one of
the most recognizable
of all dinosaurs!

WHAT'S SO SPECIAL ABOUT STEGOSAURUS?

WHEN STEGOSAURUS LIVED

JURASSIC 154 – 148 mya

TOOTH SIZE

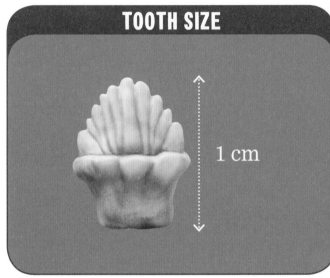

1 cm

WEIGHT

4 TONNES

FAST OR SLOW?

SPEED out of 10

2

THE BEST BITS!

DISCOVERED, SO FAR

SEVERAL
PARTIAL
SKELETONS

HOW FRIGHTENING?

SCARY

1	6
if chilling	if attacked

MEAT OR PLANTS?

SPECIAL BITS

ARMOUR PLATES

TAIL SPIKES

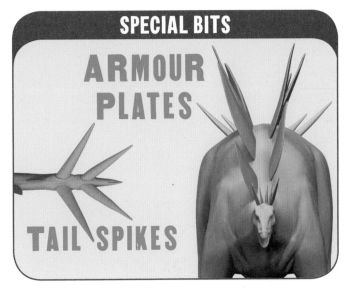

WHAT'S NEXT?

OTHER EXCITING TITLES AVAILABLE NOW!

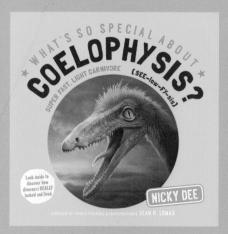

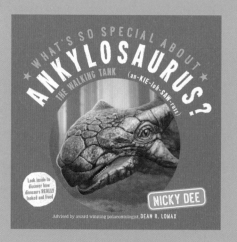

COELOPHYSIS
super-fast, light carnivore; the first skull to travel into space!

ANKYLOSAURUS
the walking tank

T. REX
the 'King of the Dinosaurs', the ultimate bone cruncher

COMING SOON

Megalosaurus
the very first dinosaur to be named

Triceratops
horned and frilled with a massive skull

Diplodocus
long necked, whip-tailed giant

Leaellynasaura
tiny, bug-eyed, long tailed Australian

Join the 'What's So Special Club'

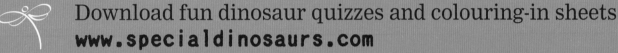

JOIN OUR FREE CLUB

Download fun dinosaur quizzes and colouring-in sheets
www.specialdinosaurs.com

Enter the exciting world of a 3D artist and discover
how a 3D dinosaur is created and made to look real!

Find out more about our experts and when they
first became fascinated by dinosaurs.

Who is Nicky Dee? Meet the author online.

Join the club and be the first to hear about
exciting new books, activities and games.

Club members will be first in line to order
new books in the series!

Copyright Published in 2016
by The Dragonfly Group Ltd

email info@specialdinosaurs.com
website www.specialdinosaurs.com

First printed in 2016
Copyright © Nicky Dee 2016
Nicky Dee has asserted her right under the
Copyright, Designs, and Patents Act 1988 to be
identified as the Author of this work.

ISBN: 978-0-9935293-1-3

Printed in China

ACKNOWLEDGEMENTS

Dean R. Lomax
talented, multiple award-winning
palaeontologist, author and science
communicator and the consultant
for the series.
www.deanrlomax.co.uk

David Eldridge
specialist book designer

Gary Hanna
thoroughly talented 3D artist

Scott Hartman
skeletons and silhouettes, professional
palaeoartist and palaeontologist

Ian Durneen
skilled digital sketch artist of the
guest dinosaurs

Ron Blakey
Colorado Plateau Geosystems Inc.
creator of the original
paleogeographic maps

My family
patient, encouraging and wonderfully
supportive. Thank you!

To find out more about our artists, designers
and illustrators please visit the website
www.specialdinosaurs.com